White Male Privilege

A Study of Racism in America
40 Years After the Voting Rights Act

Mark Rosenkranz

Law Dog
B O O K S
Pleasanton, CA

Hardcover Edition ISBN 13: 978-0-9791089-1-4

12 11 10 09 08 07   1 2 3 4 5 6

Table of Contents

1. Introduction   vii
2. Out of Sight, Out of Mind   1
3. What Color Is White?   7
4. What Color Is Privilege?   13
5. The Political History of Whiteness   17
6. What Is White Condescension?   27
7. Reflexivity: Regarding Denial   31
8. From the Outside, Looking In   43
9. Interview One – In The Past   47
10. Interview Two – Depends On Industry   49
11. Interview Three – Snow Cool   51
12. Interview Four – Silicon Valley   55
13. Interview Five – Buddy System   57
14. Interview Six – Ebonic Plague   59
15. Interview Seven – The Swann Experience   67
16. Interview Eight – An Over-Correction   77
17. Looking Back On What I Had Learned   79
18. Where Will the Future Take Us?   83

Bibliography   93

Acknowledgements

Thanks to my wife for her constant support. I would like to pass a special gratitude to my mother and father for their continual support of my vision from its infancy, and Raul Nava for guiding me through this process. I owe appreciation to Brian Swann, D.D.S. and Professor Katarin Jurich, Ph.D. for opening my eyes to the subject of racism. I also want to thank Bill Platt for believing in me enough to make this book possible.

— *Mark Rosenkranz*

Introduction

White Male Privilege has been an integral part of our American culture since those early days after the arrival of the Nina, the Pinta and the Santa Maria. In the post-Civil War and post-Civil Rights era when blacks and whites were said to have become equal, "White Male Privilege" had been declared dead, and yet, many of its incarnations are still practiced and taken for granted.

Thirty-five years after the untimely death of Martin Luther King, America still harbors and denies its racial inequities. White Male Privilege is just one profile of the global face of racism in the world today as we progress into the 21st Century. While not the most important issue America faces today, it is the one facet of racism that Americans brazenly suggest that they have overcome and left in the ashes of the past.

When we look upon the faces of our young, hope would suggest that America has overcome its past inequities to set a brighter hope upon tomorrow. But, even today, we can look upon the faces and into the eyes of our young, and we see the same racial hatreds that have plagued mankind since the ancient days of old.

It took nearly two hundred years before America could remove the government sponsorship of racism from our government institutions. And although racism has been removed from the written law of our governments, it has yet to be removed from the fabric of our American society.

While many prominent people in today's America may overstate the influence of racism in our society, many other people of prominence **deny** the subtle undercurrents of racism in our modern lives. Denial does not diminish the existence of a problem.

People of all walks of life continue to deny the existence of racism in today's America, even in the face of racially motivated assaults and murders in our streets, neighborhoods, communities, and rural areas. Although these kinds of events do not have a resonance in the news stories that they may have had forty years ago, they still do occur on a regular basis. In small town and big city America, the races fight it out. Mind you, it is not the older members of our society engaging in these conflicts rather, it is our young people meeting to spread a beating or killing in the name of racial superiority.

We, the older generations, tend to follow the path of teaching our beliefs to others, rather than stepping toe-to-toe to force our views upon another. It is far easier to pass our prejudices on to our children.

When the Civil Rights Era of the 1960's began to draw to a close, we the people finally managed to remove racial supremacy from the law books of the United States. Thus began a transition. When the law began to disregard White Male Privilege as a viable legal definition and tool of repression, white males began to shift their enforcement of the idea from government mandated rules of conduct to commonly regarded tools for corporate profit. As the white male power structure in America began the shift from government enforcement to corporate enforcement of the idea, the Civil Rights forces took their war to the boardrooms of America. The Civil Rights activists brought with them new legislation from the freshly cleansed government entities, who had previously enforced the doctrines of hate and now by law had to enforce the doctrines of equality.

With decades having passed in this battle, many Americans have come to believe that the evil genie of prejudice had finally been put back into the bottle, sealed in a concrete encasement, and dropped into the depths of the deepest ocean.

The hallways of corporate America have opened their doors to faces of all races, creeds, colors and sexes. And while on the surface it may seem like White Male Privilege has finally been defeated, it has not.

Denial is a powerful tool in the human psyche; and assumption is a more dangerous tool in the human condition. We laymen would like to believe that since our corporate corridors have been opened to all races, creeds, colors and sexes, that the White Male Privilege has finally been dealt its deathblow. We assume that we have defeated the devil — but like they say, the devil is in the details. We can assume all we want that we have finally overcome, but it does not mean that we have. Denial is the worst part of the problem. Even when we see the ugly face of prejudice in the workplace, we tend to deny its existence on account of all of the positive improvements that have occurred in the workplace over the last 100 years.

The truth is that while the glass ceiling may be way up high on the ladder to power, the glass ceiling does still exist in practice. White Male Privilege does still exist in America today.

The United States is the only country on the planet that was created with the basic premise that "all men are created equal." And we all know how that turned out, "all white men are created equal." We are fast approaching 230 years since the foundation of the United States of America, and we are still working to create an America where "all men are created equal."

Out of Sight, Out of Mind

We should not overlook the influence that White Male Privilege still holds over people here in these United States.

White Male Privilege is exercised today in ways that are subtle, rather than blatant. The purveyors of this kind of prejudice prefer to keep their actions outside of the visible arena — as they say, "out of sight, out of mind." They believe if they can hide their prejudiced behaviors, then their subordinates can continue to relish in their existence of ignorance and denial.

Unfortunately, White Male Privilege, whether hidden or

in the open, builds upon the foundation for a vicious circle of prejudices.

Prejudice in whatever form it may take will in turn create more subtle types of oppression and racism. The way I see it is that racism and oppression might not be as blatant as they used to be, but they exist and they are stronger than ever. In fact, these subtle forms of racism might even be worse in some ways, because it is a form of backstabbing.

I believe the definition of privilege is unearned given power, given to some and not to others, which influences and creates a nasty chain reactions in our society. I believe a great many people in our society simply do not see it, or do not want to see it happening around them.

White Male Privilege is the unearned privilege one is given for simply being white. As a white male in America, I have even discovered that others have bestowed the privilege upon me as well. Have I earned this privilege? No. Did I ask for this privilege? No. Do I benefit from this privilege? I am sure I do, and I am sure I always have. Does that make it right? Certainly, it does not.

To have a full appreciation of White Male Privilege, it is essential to gain an understanding of the experiences and processes of exclusion and inclusion.

The challenge for us is to take that personal journey through the experiences of others in order to become better people down the road.

The world looks much different when you are sitting inside a thing looking outward, than when you are on the outside trying to look in. If you are sitting inside of your air-conditioned home in the blazing peak of summer, it is hard to place yourself into the thoughts and feelings of the guy mowing his lawn in the sweltering heat outside. Sure, most of us can relate to the gentleman outside to a certain extent, because we have mowed our own lawn on many hot afternoons. But, if you have a gardener to take care of that unpleasant task for you, it might just be a little bit difficult to relate to the challenges of fighting off the heat, walking behind a machine that generates even more heat in your small space of the outdoors, wrestling with insects, being sprayed with small bits of cut grass, and inhaling the pollen that is filling the air around him.

Over the next few chapters, I intend to introduce you to the world outside, to bring you into the lives of people who may be outside of your own experience, people who may very well be looking toward your life from afar. I will share with you the personal stories of some people, whom I know or have met, that have sought out inclusion in our society and have been met with exclusionary tactics from the mainstream of our society.

Understanding cannot come from simply standing in another's shoes for an hour. It requires more — it takes an ability to fully appreciate the challenges met by another in everyday life. It takes more than just to tell your gardener to take an afternoon off while you mow the lawn in his stead. When you finish the lawn, you must be able to carry yourself into the whole of his life. And even that is still not enough. Most importantly, you must be able to see **your world** through his eyes.

In order to see your world through the eyes of your gardener or another, you must be able to transition yourself from "exclusionary thinking" to "inclusive thinking." To truly appreciate the life of another, you must be able to move your thoughts to the center of the life experience. Left wing and Right wing becomes Centrist. Black and white becomes human. Man and woman becomes one. From the center of our world, there are no longer two sides to an issue, but rather the universal experience of all mankind.

"Shifting the center means putting at the center of our thinking the experiences of groups who have formerly been excluded." (Anderson and Collins 1998) "Shifting the center is a shift in stance that illuminates the experiences of not only the oppressed groups but also of those in the dominant culture." (Anderson and Collins 1998)

Exclusionary thinking is a narrow way of looking at things and it excludes different points of view. Exclusionary thinking is a thought pattern that speaks to others and says, "There is my way, and there is the wrong way."

Developing inclusive thinking is more than just "understanding diversity," it is a way to construct new analyses that focus on the centrality of the experiences of us all. (Anderson and Collins 1998)

As we move forward in this book, it may just come to pass that in the end, we can all make the transition from exclusive thinking to inclusive thinking. And hopefully in the end, we will become better people for our journey.

What Color Is White?

"Rarely in this country do we identify ourselves or each other as white." It is an adjective, which is not heard explicitly, but is implied. Let me give you some examples.

Read the following lines: "He walked into the room and immediately noticed her." "The average American drinks two cups of coffee a day." "Women today want to catch a man who is strong, but sensitive." Are all these people white? Read the sentences again and imagine the people referred to are Chinese Americans. Does that change the meaning? How about if these people were black or Native Americans?" (Uprooting racism 1996)

The way the human mind manages incoming information is interesting. It has long been noted that people like other people who are most like themselves. The more successful writers are those who understand that they should give definition to their characters and events without giving too many intimate details. Writers who utilize this approach are able to make connections on an almost universal level, because they are allowing the reader to use his or her own imagination to fill in the finer details of the story. Each reader will interpret the story in a way that more closely represents the reader's view of the world.

The generic statement, he walked into the room and immediately noticed her... will be interpreted by the reader in a way that most closely represents the reader's own life situations. If the reader is Caucasian and the reader spends most of life associating him or herself with Caucasians, the reader will automatically make the "he" and "she" in the story white, unless the writer has given a previous indication of some definition that is more specific and different. If the reader is of Asian origin and only spends life in the company of other Asians, then the reader will naturally define the "he" and "she" as of Asian descent.

This might seem obvious, but it is not. It is very important to realize that our color and race influence our own perspectives toward others and others toward us.

The start of realizing White Male Privilege is in acknowledging the fact that many white males are given privilege over others. Let us return to the previous statement "It has long been noted that people like other people who are most like themselves." White men have always held positions of power and influence in America, and those in the power structure have always passed power on to others who are most like themselves.

Introspection is a vital step in beginning to appreciate and understand the nature of White Male Privilege. As with anything in life, the surest step to understanding the lives, the decisions, and the choices of others, is first learning to understand why you do what you do.

People of color are made aware that they are people of color every day. The first step from exclusion to inclusion is to carry ones own whiteness with them. What difference does it make being white? What does being white really feel like? This concept came to me when a black man told a white professor that he never goes a day without thinking of the fact that he is black. "Whatever our economic status, most of us become paralyzed with some measure of fear, guilt, anger, defensiveness or confusion if we are named as white when racism is being addressed."

Does saying that we are being white make us feel guilty of being a racist or traitorous toward other whites? (Uprooting Racism 1996)

The point I am trying to make is that it is equally important to see that "whiteness" is a color too. This is one of the first steps toward realizing the existence of this privilege. How can one know someone else without first knowing themselves? Before we can identify with others, we need to identify with ourselves.

What Color is Privilege?

At this point, it is important to define what "privilege" is exactly. According to Webster's New World dictionary (1988), "privilege" is defined as:

1. A right, advantage favor, or immunity specially granted to one especially, a right held by certain individual, group, or class and withheld from certain others or all others.

"Privileges are the economic 'extras' that those of us who are middle class and wealthy gain at the expense of poor and working class people of all races." (Uprooting Racism 1996).

Being a white male has its privileges...

- We can usually count on police protection rather than being harassed by them.
- White males are given more attention, respect and status in conversations than people of color.
- We tend to see people who look like us in the media, history books, news and music in a positive light.
- White males have more recourse to and credibility within the legal system.
- White males do not have to represent their race.
- Most of the time what we do is not qualified, limited, discredited or acclaimed simply because of our racial background.
- White males will be paid $1.00 for every $.60 that a person of color makes.

There are other economic benefits too.

"All the land in this country was taken from Native Americans. Much of the infrastructure of this country was built by slave labor, incredibly low-paid labor, or by prison labor performed by men and women of color." " Further property and material goods were appropriated by whites through the colonization of the west and Southwest throughout the 19th century, through the internment of Japanese Americans during World War II, through racial riots against people of color in the 18th, 19th and 20th centuries, and through an ongoing legacy of legal manipulation and exploitation." The low income, the low paying and the dangerous jobs that people of color have are because of these variables. (Uprooting Racism 1996)

The Political History of Whiteness

In order to truly understand White Male Privilege, we must also look at the politics of privilege, and we must rediscover our knowledge of the history of privilege.

Even "citizenship was a racially inscribed concept at the outset" of the foundation of the United States. "By an act of Congress, only 'free white' immigrants could be naturalized." "Doing justice to both the 'whiteness' and the 'racial distinctness' of the immigrant saga will prove difficult enough under any circumstances, so accustomed have we become to thinking of race as color." (Whiteness of A Different Color, 1999)

The nineteenth-century antagonism between the English and the Irish was, at the time, a racial conflict between Anglo-Saxons and Celts. Having immigrated to North America, many Celts took on a new racial identity, and participated in the politics of white supremacy groups like "The Order of Caucasians," alongside the Anglo-Saxons who denied the Celts equality in the streets of Boston.

"The Order of Caucasians" rose to prominence in the California of the 1870's in an attempt to institutionalize discrimination against the Chinese through the political system. Many historians refer to the movement that served as the group's defining campaign, the "*Extermination of the Chinaman in San Francisco*." Politicians throughout the western United States campaigned in Washington D.C. in an attempt to establish laws to slow or stop the "*invasion of Mongolians*," at the national level. Initially, they hoped to legalize Chinese exclusion, and then they moved to exclusion campaigns against the Japanese in later years.

When the Celts came to America, the Anglo-Saxons were in control of the American political environment. The Celts were the low-man on the totem pole throughout the northeastern United States. In those days, there was "white" (Anglo-Saxon), and then there was the other "white" meat (Celtic). Although both races were "white" in appearance, the law treated them each differently — one was "included" and the other was "excluded." The Celts needed to reinvent themselves as Caucasians... and they found a way. When a Celtic man joined any organization, the form he filled out defined the races: Caucasian, Negro, Indian, Chinese, etc. It was a rather simple process by the Celts to change their lot in life from "excluded" to "included;" they simply joined an organization and checked the box that said "Caucasian."

"Whiteness" has indeed posed many serious problems when it comes to narrating the European immigrant saga to the United States. Let's take a look at this specifically.

The people who migrated from Europe were from Norway, Germany, England, Italy, and many other countries, were generally considered "white" or "Caucasian." They were all people who came from different political systems and socio-economic systems. Just as the conflict between the Anglo-Saxons and the Celts demonstrated, there were many different kinds of white people. There were many different kinds of whiteness.

"The demographics of the republic began to change dramatically in the mid-nineteenth century. In the early decades of the republic, immigration had been calculated by the mere thousands per year — an influx of 8,385 from all sending countries combined in the year 1820, for instance. But these yearly figures climbed to the tens of thousands per year by the mid-1820s, and to the hundreds of thousands per year by the 1840s." By 1847 immigration from Ireland leaped to 234,968. By 1855, 3,031,339 immigrants came ashore in the United States. Of these, 976,711 were from Germany.

"Over the next several decades the economic and po-litical dislocations across Europe continued to send in-creasing numbers of migrants to American shores, with each region furnishing its own statistical curve of migra-tion slopes and peaks: Irish migration peaked at 221,253 in 1851; German migration peaked at 250,630 in 1882; Italian migration peaked at 285,731 in 1907; and Rus-sian (largely Jewish) migration peaked at 258,943 also in 1907." (Whiteness of a Different Color 1999) These statistics show how even the white population in the United States is a melting pot in itself.

These immigration figures have always influenced the landscape of American politics. And, white males have played a very important role regarding politics in America, because federal law has always guaranteed their voting power. The white male stood alone in the voting booth until the latter half of the 19th century.

Of course, even though the 15th Amendment (ratified in 1870) of the United States Constitution guaranteed a vote for black Americans, African-Americans never really enjoyed full and equal voting rights until the Voting Rights Act was passed a century later in 1965. By the 1890's, many southern states had implemented various and rigorous voter registration laws, which included literacy tests and poll taxes among other things. These voter registration laws although concocted using race-neutral language, were intended to keep black citizens out of the voting booth, excluding them from equal participation in the political process.

With the passage of the 19th Amendment to the U.S. Constitution in 1920, women finally earned the right to vote. For all intents and purposes, the government sponsored White Male Privilege in the voting booth was not fully eradicated until 1965.

The erosion of White Male Privilege began in 1860 when Abraham Lincoln declared war on the South. Lincoln's dream found legs to stand on, in 1865, when the northern armies defeated the south. The white male's control of the voting process came in 1870, followed by the final step in 1920.

Under a movement that began in the days of John F. Kennedy, brought to life by Martin Luther King, and signed into federal law by Lyndon B. Johnson, African-Americans gained their full voting rights as intended by the 17th Amendment to the U.S. Constitution.

Two measures were taken to make this final step. The first step was the passage of the 24th Amendment to the U.S. Constitution, which prohibited the use of a poll tax to exclude American citizens from the voting process. The final step was the Voting Rights Act of 1965, which prohibited literacy tests or any other type of testing designed to exclude members of the American public from exercising their legal right to vote. On August 6th, 1965, the ultimate control of the American political process was officially transitioned to "include" all Americans, regardless or race, color, previous condition of servitude, or sex.

From its inception, the United States had discriminated between people based on their skin color. Even today, forty years beyond the Voting Rights Act of 1965, there remains a widespread belief, that "individualism" and "equality of opportunity" has always been and is still greater in white America than anywhere else.

The start of White Male Privilege began hundreds of years ago, when slavery was brought to the shores of America, from sea to shining sea. Certainly, racism did not begin in America. We have seen evidence of racism through the millenniums, even into the Old Testament and to the time of Moses when the Egyptians subjugated the Jews.

White males in the upper socio-economic classes have always been encouraged to get a college education. College was their way to keep themselves above those whom they intended to serve them.

"The treatment of blacks has been for the most part, a deviation from the American Creed throughout the history of the republic. If we count American History as starting around 1600, blacks have been here almost from the beginning. However, they spent their first two and a half centuries as slaves. For a hundred years after 1865 they largely served as a lower-caste group working under explicit or implicit Jim Crow policies, with little opportunity to gain educational or financial resources. Caste systems — slavery or segregation — were much more explicitly hierarchical and hereditary than European feudalism. Blacks have only been given a claim to political equality and economic opportunity since the 1960's." (American Exceptionalism)

It must be said that there could be many more points using other cultures as examples, even by emphasizing the Chinese and Japanese immigrants in California during the late 1800's in the days of "The Order of Caucasians." But, my focus on the black culture is being emphasized to make a point.

"The white American value system has emphasized the individual. Citizens have been expected to demand and protect their rights on a personal basis." "The experience of black Americans, however, has focused on group characteristics defining and treating people not according to their personal merits but according to their ancestry, their race and their ethnic group." (American Exceptionalism 1996)

Black Washington Post columnist, William Raspberry, made an interesting and compelling argument. "White Americans... do not see themselves as racist, or opponents of equal opportunity and fundamental fairness. What they are opposed to, are the efforts to provide preferential benefits for minorities. How could we (blacks) expect them to buy a product we spent 400 years trying to have recalled: race-based advantages enshrined into law?"

What is White Condescension?

"White condescension" can be defined in a few ways. First of all, Webster's New World Dictionary defines "condescension" as the following:

1. act or instance of condescending;
2. a patronizing manner of behavior.

Professor Shelby Steele defines white condescension this way: "Whites bend over backward to show their good motives and unbiased minds. This provides a way of regaining the moral authority lost, due to slavery and Jim Crow."

"Economics professor, Walter Williams 'bases white condescension on the emotional and irrational white guilt...

That whites feel, if not personally, at least responsible by heritage for the black plight.' Thus Williams offers universal amnesty to whites so that white people can quit acting like damn fools." (The Ten Things You Can't Say In America, Larry Elder 2000)

"White condescension" is a very important thing to take a look at regarding White Male Privilege, because it has some underlying themes which I am going to discuss. First of all, white condescension does a lot of damage to whites, blacks and all races. In fact, white condescension does its greatest damage to society as a whole, because it inhibits society's growth potential in terms of its moral existence.

White condescension, basically says to a child, the rules used by other ethnic and immigrant groups do not apply to you. "Forget about work hard, get an education, and possess good values. No, for you, we'll alter the rules by lowering the standards and expecting less. Expect less, get less." What passes as white compassion, is just plain white condescension. (The Ten Things You Can't Say In America 2000)

Reflexivity: Regarding Denial

"**Reflexivity**" is the noun for "**reflexive**," which according to Webster's New World Dictionary 1988 means: designating or expressing a grammatical relation in which a verb's subject and an object in the sentence refer to the same person or thing, serving to indicate that the action of the verb is directed back to the subject.

"**Denial**" according to Webster's New World Dictionary 1988 means

1. the act of denying: a saying "no" (to a request, demand, etc.);
2. a statement in opposition to another; contradiction, (the denial of a rumor.)

A very important element of White Male Privilege is the denial of it, either "with" or "without" awareness. People in denial believe that discrimination is a thing of the past. These people believe that there is equal opportunity for all, and they believe that now there is an equal playing field.

Just the other day I went to my daughters Girl Scout awards ceremony. We all stood up and said the pledge of allegiance. When we spoke the last words, "for liberty and justice for all," I thought to myself, "just because something is said doesn't mean that it is reality."

As a country we live with these principles, which is a good thing; however, how about the people for which there isn't any justice? How about the Native Americans that lost so much more than just their land, which in itself was horrifying? How about the blacks and the centuries of slavery?

How about the Japanese that had to stay in interment camps during World War II, most of whom lost all of their possessions and freedoms simply because they were descended from Japanese immigrants? Why didn't we also intern all of the German-Americans during World War II? The list goes on and on and on. How about all the discrimination that exists against women today?

White males have all directly benefited from these oppressive behaviors. It's no wonder it is so hard for white males to be "inclusive" in their thinking. Reality can hurt when you really take a good look at it.

Denial takes a lot of its strength from **minimization**. "Today we continue to minimize racism by saying, personal achievement mostly depends on personal ability. Racism isn't prevalent anymore or (about slavery) there were a lot of kind slave owners." (Uprooting racism 1996)

"Native Americans were killed and their land taken. In response we say, a few Indians died because they didn't

have immunity to European diseases. We try to minimize the presence of the 12-15 million Native Americans in North America prior to 1492 and to minimize
the violence we committed toward them." (Uprooting
racism1996)

What gets me about all this is that people today emphasize the distance of the history of the events, and people
argue loudly that "they" need to move on with their lives.
Well, I agree that people need to move on with their
lives, however, it's important to realize that it is not always that easy.

Racism in its many forms has been strengthening other
prejudices for centuries. Some families harbored a grow-
ing anger towards their oppressors. Some families cow-
ered in the corner believing that they were not as good
as their oppressors. The teaching of the parents were
passed on and strengthened in the children, in most
cases. Now and again, a rebellious child would take the
exact opposite stance to the teachings of his or her par-

ents.

When fear of and submission to the oppressor are passed from parent to child for several generations, it is difficult for a new generation to break from the teachings of their childhood. When hatred of the oppressor is taught from the age of awareness, hate is a difficult master to conquer. The child grows up and passes his biases and beliefs to his or her own children, who pass those feelings to their own children. It is a never-ending cycle.

Just like the Klansman who cannot stop preaching hate to his children, and just like the average Joe next door who distrusts Arabs, the shackles of racism are not so easily removed.

To emphasize my point, let us take a moment to step away from the questions of racism and racial prejudices and fears. Let's step into a world that is a bit more personal to each of us.

Think back to your childhood. Think about the relationship you had with your parents.

Do you have your thoughts gathered? Good.

What is the one thing that stands out in your mind as the one, most memorable thing about the relationship you had with your parents?

For some people, they will say, "my parents supported me in everything that I did. They were my very best friends."

Other people will not have memories quite so fond. Others will remember most painfully the put-downs and the statements made that hurt the child inside of them.

Which group do you belong to?

Whichever group you belong to, you can clearly feel the joy or the pain that your parents passed on to you. You can feel it as if it happened only yesterday.

How old are you now?

Have you been able to shake off the influences of your parents? Do you still experience times in your life where you are exactly the person that your parents told you that you are, all those years ago?

Right or wrong, our parents instilled in us feelings of good and/or bad. Good or bad, we all will have moments where our parent's words will influence our decisions in a way that is contrary to who we are today.

So, many of us still carry with us baggage from our childhoods. Of course, we don't want to admit to that, because we are now adults, and we are in full control of our lives.

Denial is the drug of choice for most of us. We deny that those words said to us ten, twenty, thirty, forty, even seventy years ago by our parents, can still make our hearts grieve or to cause us to lash out in anger.

So, let's return to our discussion.

If you still carry baggage from your childhood, in your psychological make-up, why should "they," the descendants of the oppressed be any different from you?

A significant part of your psyche is straight from the mouths of your parents, and so is the psyche of the person you want to "move on with **their** lives."

It is always easier to pass on the "responsibility" for something to other people. While we may proudly take responsibility for some things in our lives, we have all been guilty at one time or another of trying to pass responsibility for something to another. Let's face it; this is one of the commonalities that unite the human race. Everything that is wrong in the world is someone else's fault.

Blame is another factor of White Male Privilege that needs to be considered. Today we blame other cultures and races for racism by saying, "Look at the way they act." "If they weren't so angry..." Or, "They are immoral, lazy, dumb, or unambitious." (Uprooting racism 1996)

When someone blames someone for something, they are not focusing on themselves. They are "looking from the outside in," instead of "from the inside out." It is much more difficult to look from the inside out, because a person might discover things about themselves that they did not want to know.

Having the ability to view the world "from the inside out" can bring clarity to one's life. Introspection is crucial for the transformation from exclusive to inclusive thinking.

Earlier, I had said that the United States is a melting pot. Lot's of people say it everyday. But, pure and simple, that is an oversimplification. I am reiterating that statement here to show you my own biases.

Another reason why White Male Privilege is allowed to perpetuate it's self, is because we do not acknowledge the unintentional hurt it inflicts upon others. "We know that the complete elimination of Native Americans from the United States was government policy as well part of the general everyday discourse of white Americans." (Uprooting Racism 1996)

What a powerful statement!

What is so sad is that there are millions of Americans that do not even give it a thought. Today, there is a world-wide Aids epidemic — especially in South Africa, however our "United States is not helping that country like we could be. Why? We are not aware of it from the inside. Sure, we are from the outside looking in, but that is not sufficient for empathy to exist.

"Today we continue to claim that racism is unintentional by saying discrimination may happen, but most people are well intentioned. (Uprooting Racism 1996) Through my fieldwork, many people dodged personal responsibility for perpetuating White Male Privilege and racism by saying, "White Male Privilege is no longer an issue."

"To broaden our narrow thinking which constrains our worldview and understanding, we need to promote the thinking, creative expression and leadership of people of color. We should do this not because the result will be better than white thinking, but because we have systematically controlled, historic responsibility to work for the end of white cultural, political and economic exploitation." (Uprooting Racism 1996)

"Awareness of social injustice caused by privilege of class, race, gender, and religion, is just the first step toward social equality and justice. All men are created equal in the sight of God. Freedom is never free. Social Justice must be fought for." (Francine Armstrong)

From The Outside, Looking In

It is never enough to stand on your own convictions, regarding a topic as important as this one. I felt it was important to gain an understanding of White Male Privilege from several points of view to ensure that I would be able to give this topic due diligence.

During this process, I was able to gain personal interviews with several people who see White Male Privilege in their everyday lives.

I also spoke to people who did not have any idea of what White Male Privilege was.

I conducted interviews with eight different people, (taped with their permission), which showed how their perspectives on this topic varied widely.

I consider myself fortunate enough to have been able to interview Brian Swann, brother of the famous footballer, Lynn Swann. In 1974, Brian Swann, his brother Lynn, a third brother Calvin, and a cousin, Michael Henderson, found themselves caught up events that should never have taken place.

Lynn Swann may have been famous in those days — and he was known personally by one of the police officers involved in the whole affair — but his notoriety did not keep him from being falsely accused and falsely arrested in a racially motivated incident. In the aftermath of the whole incident, the Swann's successfully won a civil-right's lawsuit against the San Francisco Police Department concerning the events that took place that fateful day.

I interviewed Brian Swann in 2000, as I was preparing the transcript for this book. He shares with us in great detail the events that happened that day in San Francisco, and he shares his views on White Male Privilege in modern-day America.

After you are finished reading Brian's personal story, you might see the spark that may have led Lynn Swann to seek out political office. As I was finishing this book, it came to my attention that Lynn was contemplating a run for Governor in the great State of Pennsylvania. As we were ready to take this book to press, the Associated Press reported that Lynn Swann likely has enough votes to secure the GOP nomination on February 11, 2006, for the Governor's race in Pennsylvania.
(http://www.sfgate.com/cgi-bin/article.cgi?file=/n/a/ 2006/02/01/politics/p073827S86.DTL)

Interview 1 – In The Past

In my first interview, I spoke with a young Hispanic male in his mid-twenties who believed that White Male Privilege existed in the past, but he felt that society had pretty much erased it from modern-day life.

He said, "It used to be that way." And, then he said, "I don't think its that way any more."

Interview 2 – Depends On Industry

Another Hispanic male in his mid twenties said, "it depends on what type of industry you are going into."

In his viewpoint, it was not necessarily an idea of white males exerting privilege over another. Instead, he felt that the supposed White Male Privilege was an issue of what kinds of work environments white males are willing to endure to bring home a paycheck.

He gave an example, "Like in construction, ninety five percent of the people are Mexican, because they are willing to work non-stop hours." He said, "White people won't do that."

Interview 3 – Snow Cool

In my third interview, I spoke with was a black woman who was twenty-four years of age.

When I asked her about White Male Privilege, she said that she first noticed it in elementary school. "The differences in privileges that the white kids had over me came through in the teaching. Teachers were very, um... they favored the little white boys and the white girls more than they favored me."

She gave an example of when she auditioned for a school play. She was up for the part of Snow White and only when her parents stepped in, was she given the part. The schoolteacher as a final affront changed the name of Snow White to "Snow Cool," in the school play.

She went on to say that White Male Privilege is becoming more of a power play issue, because more minorities are moving up in the corporate world. She mentioned that she has seen several minorities in positions of authority and corporate management. But, she felt that they were exceptions to the rule, rather than examples of good corporate ethics and an environment of social equality.

...I have got to admit something to you.

When I heard the story about "Snow Cool," I was floored. She wanted to play the part of "Snow White"; she did not sign up to play in a "minstrel show" meant to demean her own race!

To learn more about the history of the "minstrel show," go to this website: http://www.musicals101.com/minstrel.htm

Racism is wrong pure, and simple. But, when the stain of racism is thrown upon a young, impressionable child that is more than just wrong! It is an affront to everything that America is supposed to stand for!

It is bad enough when racism is allowed to fester in Corporate America, but when it happens in our schools, we are in a world of hurt.

Interview 4 – Silicon Valley

My fourth interview was conducted with a woman in her mid- to late-thirties who held positions in the corporate world.

She said she had observed White Male Privilege on a regular basis. She mostly noticed this behavior in corporate meetings, although she did note, "the corporate world is changing somewhat."

When asked why she thought the corporate environment was starting to change, she suggested that it was changing because of an influx of "non-white" males entering the corporate environment in Silicon Valley, where she worked.

She also stated that there were also certain white males, in positions of power, who embraced racial equality in the workplace. She felt that their influence was having a positive effect on the whole corporate culture.

Interview 5 – Buddy System

A black male in his early-twenties felt that White Male Privilege was more closely related to the "buddy system."

He started his interview with the statement, "White Male Privilege goes hand in hand with the glass ceiling."

I thought this individual had great insight into the human condition when he said, "people in positions of power want to promote individuals who more closely resembles themselves, rather than someone who is different than them."

This young man stated that he has seen several incidents, where people who have the "actual skills and talent level" to get the job done, are "passed over, denied and overlooked" for promotions, because they don't look like their bosses. Far too often, he has seen people of lesser qualifications get the job, because he felt that they more closely resembled the person who made the final promotion decision.

This young man concluded by saying "it's going to take a lot to over come that kind of bias."

Interview 6 – Ebonic Plague

To balance the discussion, I turned to a Caucasian gentleman who was 40 years old at the time of our interview. He started by saying that he was going to say some things that are "very controversial."

My interview with him lived up to his promise. His ideas are controversial. They were even controversial when Bill Cosby shared ideas very similar to what this individual had said.
I will talk about Bill Cosby's comments further after this interview.

In his interview, this gentleman said that he did not believe that White Male Privilege is as much of a problem as it once was. "I don't think *we* have predominant privilege, I think we have a structure set up now that anybody can have privilege now."

To frame his ideas, he introduced a new phrase, "ebonic-plague."

Just to *make sure that I did not misunderstand him*, he said, **"Not the bubonic plague, the ebonic-plague for our black friends."**

Yes, he got my attention.

He said that he does not deny that there is a racism problem, but he does not think it is as predominant as it was thirty years ago.

He expressed the idea that "If you look around and you see the successful black people in our society, there seems to be a commonality between them, and it's not the color of their skin. Their commonality is their ability to speak properly."

He continued, there is "equal opportunity right now for everybody to succeed, but one of the things that I believe we have to do is to let go of ebonics, and study very, very hard. We have to study very hard, to learn how to speak intelligently."

Interestingly, he added, "This goes not only for blacks, but for whites." He stated, "White people too," who can't get good jobs, "typically don't get the job, because they don't speak very well."

He argues that racism is not the actual cause. Instead, the real blame resides in the poor communication skills of those who feel oppressed.

In his observations, he stated, "Some of our black families continue with this 'chip on the shoulder problem', which says that everything that is wrong in the world, is still because of the white guy."

He lamented that "mothers and fathers raise their black children to resent white people. And, that gets into the subconscious of their children, who grow up to blame everything on the white people."

He said that many black families raise children who believe "that racism is the excuse for everything that goes wrong in their lives." He suggested that black people have been conditioned to believe that if something goes wrong, then you should "Just go back to racism. That's it. It is not the result of something they have done or have not done. It is not their inability or unwillingness to do what is necessary, to accomplish their goals. It is always racism."

He expressed the idea that, "Anything they can't do, because of their subconscious conditioning through their parents, is a function of racism."

He stopped for a moment, and then he said that he resented the fact that black people wanted to hang the blame for their inability to succeed on his shoulders. He resented that black families trained their children to not take responsibility for all that is good or bad in their lives.

Arguing for recognition of the progress we have made in the last forty years, he acknowledged, "Educational opportunities may not have been available to black students in the fifties, but they are available now for anyone who wants to take advantage of them."

As we concluded our interview, this gentleman was gently encouraging people to reach beyond their condition. He stated that, "I feel black families should start to program positive things." He wanted everyone to know that they "can succeed," if they work hard, study hard, and speak well.

The following is taken from an article titled "Three Cheers for Bill Cosby," and written by Walter Williams on June 2, 2004, in **Capitalism Magazine**. The following excerpts are taken from: http://www.capmag.com/article.asp?ID=3719

Walter Williams talked about Bill Cosby's speech at a gathering commemorating the *50th anniversary of the 1954 U.S. Supreme Court school desegregation decision in Brown vs. Board of Education.*

Mr. Williams stated, "For years, I've argued that most of the problems many black Americans face today have little or nothing to do with racial discrimination." Continuing, he said, "The most devastating problems encountered by a large segment of the black community are self-inflicted. Bill Cosby mentioned several of them, such as black parents who'll buy their children expensive clothing rather than something educational, poor language spoken by many children and adults, and criminals who prey on the overwhelmingly law-abiding residents of black neighborhoods."

Mr. Williams described how Bill Cosby's comments garnered applause from many members of the audience, but inspired irate responses from America's black leadership.

Thomas Sowell was quoted in the article as saying, "Bill Cosby and the black 'leadership' represent two long-standing differences about how to deal with the problems of the black community. The 'leaders' are concerned with protecting the image of blacks, while Cosby is trying to protect the future of blacks, especially those of the younger generation."

In retrospect, the comments acquired during my interview are not far different from the comments made by these individuals, who have each earned a great deal of respect in the black community.

Walter Williams echoed some of the statements made

by the "controversial" white male I interviewed.

Mr. Williams strongly argued, "Don't give me any of that legacy-of-slavery nonsense unless you can explain why all of these problems were not worse during the late 19th and early 20th centuries, at a time when blacks were much closer to slavery, were much poorer, faced more discrimination and had fewer opportunities."

You can read Walter Williams full article here: http://www.capmag.com/article.asp?ID=3719

He was very well spoken.

Mr. Williams closed his comments with the following, "Bill Cosby's bold comments might be what's necessary to get an honest and fruitful discussion going within the black community, and for that, we all owe him thanks."

Interview 7 – The Swann Experience

In the course of developing this book, I had the plea-
sure of being able to interview Brian Swann. I have
known Brian for several years.

A college-educated professional, Brian is also the
brother of famous footballer, Lynn Swann. Ordinarily, his
famous brother would not be of any importance in this
story. But, in the course of my interview, Brian shared a
personal experience related to the topic of this book, in
which his brother Lynn, his brother Calvin, and his cousin
Michael Henderson were present.

I began my interview with him by asking his opinions

about White Male Privilege. I found his thoughts on the matter to be very enlightening from a historical perspective.

Brian started off by suggesting that White Male Privilege in America began many centuries ago.

He suggested that as European colonization began in America, farmers found themselves facing labor shortages. In order to grow their farms and to build their new country, the settlers needed skilled and unskilled laborers. The problem the American colonists had was, "that as Christians, they could not conceivably take another people into slavery only for economic gain."

"Spin doctors" is actually fairly new terminology in the English language. But the activity has existed all the way back through human history. Just as the winners of a conflict get the privilege of writing the history books, those who face great challenges always seek to change the way an issue is viewed by the public. And, those early days in the New World were no different.

They needed to put a new spin on the issue of slavery in the New World.

"Therefore the philosophy of racism was born, and that is to tell the African people or the Europeans to tell themselves rather, that the African people were not human, that the African people were subhuman, and therefore justifying slavery."

Brian further stated, "The Africans were looked upon as a very suitable group of simple minded people who did not mind going into slavery, who possessed the skills necessary to cultivate and farm the New World."

As time went on some white slave owners were having sexual relations with some of the slave women and that's when the "subhuman concept" went out the window, because these slave owners could not justify having relations with their subhuman slaves. "Therefore, we became known as being human, but not sophisticated enough to take care of ourselves, and thereby needing slavery as a 'guiding philosophy' to keep us from harming ourselves and helping us to survive."

Before I share with you Brian's personal story of racism in action, I am going to give you some background information.

In the mid-1970's, in the San Francisco Bay area, there was a manhunt in progress. The Swann incident "happened to be a time when the police were in patrols looking for four black males that were suspects in the murders called the Zebra Murders, in which white Americans had been assassinated by a group of black males."

Four black Muslims were later arrested and convicted in relation to the killings of a dozen white people, between 1972 and 1974.

I have read two separate accounts of how the murders came to be known as the Zebra Murders. In one account, the San Francisco police task force, assigned to the case, was utilizing the "Z" or "Zebra" channel for communication. Another account suggested that they were called the Zebra Murders on account of the "black on white" modus operandi of the killers.

The San Francisco Police Department later admitted that they had pulled over and questioned more than 600 black men in 1974, during the course of their search for the "Zebra Killers."

Shortly after Lynn Swann had been selected as the #1 draft pick by the Pittsburgh Steelers in 1974, the Swann family went out for a celebratory dinner at a San Francisco restaurant.

Brian said that Lynn had been given an award two weeks earlier, for being the top athlete on the west coast. As part of that recognition, Lynn Swann was given a "credit card to eat with (a specific restaurant) indefinitely, with as many people as he wanted, for the rest of his life."

The Swann family took in dinner at this restaurant, and as they were leaving the restaurant, they drove down Union Avenue and were "stopped by the police for going through a yellow light."

One brother received a ticket for a torn license because the number on it couldn't be read. (In those days licenses were made of paper.) Then the brothers got out of the car and "asked the question 'why a ticket for a mutilated drivers license' and that's when the incident heated up."

One of the two police officers involved in the stop had been a "schoolmate" of Brian Swann. They knew each other. Brian knew that the officer had been to Vietnam, and he knew that he was also a gymnast. The police officer that had been Brian's schoolmate had not spoken a single word during the entire incident up until this point, other than to ask for identification.

The officer who had issued the ticket asked everyone to get back into the car.

The brothers turned to get back into the car. As they were doing so, the officer whom Brian had gone to school with, "had his Billy club out and ran after my cousin to hit him as he got into the car."

Brian said, "My brother Lynn, who has quick reflexes, turned around, saw this happening, and snatched the Billy club straight out of his hand without any pressure, and he had thrown it down the street. The police officer went berserk at that point trying to get his gun out."

The brothers "constrained him by just holding him, his arms pinned to his sides, talking to him the whole time asking him to calm down. He never said a word; he just began to struggle."

The other officer went to call for back up, and the Zebra patrol showed up in force.

Brian explained that they were relieved when backup arrived. They let loose the irate officer, and they all felt that cooler heads would prevail.

Brian said, "the resolution was that they began to beat us in the street with clubs, they kicked me in the side of the face as they handcuffed me from the back, and they just pulverized us in the street."

Brian indicated that arrest was not the end of the abuse. He said, the officers "put us in the patty wagon where they would drive twenty five feet, slam on the brakes, drive another twenty five feet, and swerve the vehicle back and forth."

The police took the Swann cousin and brothers to the police station and then beat them some more.

I have chosen to leave out the more graphic details of Brian's interview, because honestly, I just found parts of the story to be so offensive.

All of the Swann's were charged with assault and battery with a deadly weapon. The trial lasted a week and a half. The Swann's were acquitted of criminal charges.

Taking into account an appeal, the civil trial lasted nine years in which there was "nominal compensation." The Swann's were awarded $40,000 in the suit filed against the San Francisco Police Department, for the violation of their civil rights.

The police officers were each awarded $8,000 each in their counter-lawsuit against the Swann's.

Brian believes that if hadn't been for the celebrity status

of his brother, Lynn's money from the signing bonus, and the people who cared about Lynn playing football, "we would have fried like so many guys do who are afraid and plead guilty." Brian said, "once you get into the system, you are always a suspect."

Brian concluded the interview by saying "it's all about fear and keeping people in their place." He contends that "if you even the playing field between the races, then there would be balance, and people would not need to keep this mindset."

Interview 8 – An Over-Correction

In this interview, I spoke with a white male in his early-forties.

He felt that "White Male Privilege began to be addressed back in the civil rights movement, and I think it was over corrected for." He honestly believes that the over correction was affecting his own ability to find employment. Even with his master's degree in hand, he said he could not get a job.

He told me "women with my similar skills above and below me were getting job offers right and left."

He felt that there is "institutionalized bias toward white males in such a way that job descriptions were written in such a way that white males were basically not welcome to apply."

He said he had "no patience for anybody complaining about White Male Privilege. I know it exists in a legal setting and it needs to be corrected, but in a job setting it is a hollow and completely invalid argument."

Looking Back On What I Had Learned

I have lived a sheltered life regarding White Male Privilege.

I had always known that it was a factor in the lives of others. But, I had failed to properly appreciate how much of an influence it had in my own life and in the lives of others.

A novel thought had come to me at one time. I had always prided myself on the idea that I was not a prejudiced person. Then one day, I was struck with the thought that yes, yes I was. I was prejudiced against prejudiced people. I could no longer live in denial. I finally realized how important it was to be aware of White Male Privilege, in order to fully understand my own biases.

I had undertaken these eight interviews to better understand the nature of White Male Privilege, through the eyes of others — from the outside looking in, rather than from the inside looking outward. At the conclusion of many of these interviews, I felt deeply in my heart the pain that White Male Privilege brought to the lives of the people I interviewed.

Most of the people I met, during the process of bringing this book to print, had deep convictions. They just wanted to express themselves. Although the person presented in the very first interview did not seem to have much to say regarding White Male Privilege, his nonverbal behavior told a different story. I could just see it in his eyes. He definitely had feelings that went beyond the words that he spoke. Had someone other than a white male interviewed him, he might have said a whole lot more than he actually did.

I do not believe that there are any simple answers to the problems of racism and White Male Privilege, but a few recurring principles seem to have appeared over and over again in my research.

1. Education gives people the power to raise themselves to a better position.
2. The way a person speaks indicates his or her level of education, and will greatly affect the person's prospects in life.
3. Prejudices, racism and hatred are often passed on from parent to child, and will affect the beliefs of the child through its lifetime.
4. Denial and condescending attitudes allow for a more subtle form or racism to continue to flourish.
5. Racism has always been a tool used by the powerful to inflict subjugation upon other people.
6. The winners in history always have the power to rewrite the history books, to create a new spin

and an excuse for their poor behaviors towards others.

7. The only persons in life that you can truly teach the principles of equality are to you and your children.

Where Will The Future Take Us?

As we entered the new millennium, our hopes were strong and bright. We could see enlightenment and equality on the horizon fast approaching.

Then, in September of 2001, our hopes were dashed on the rocks. We could not understand how other people around the world could hate us so very much. We could not understand why Palestinians cheered in the streets for the devastation that had come to our shores. We could not understand how some of the people of the Muslim world could teach their children to hate us.

Our eyes were finally opened to others who hate everything that we believe to be righteous and true. They hate our values and our way of life. Our eyes were opened to the beliefs of people around the world who do not see us through the same eyes that we view ourselves.

We were shocked to see people who openly teach hatred of Americans to their children, in schools and in mosques. We just could not believe that they could not see us as we see ourselves. It was a real shock to our belief systems.

On that September day in New York City, the racially divided citizenry of the Big Apple came together as one. If even just for a day, New Yorkers were not black, white, Hispanic, Latino, Jewish or Irish; they were New Yorkers. They were Americans. They were one people.

Subtle, racial divides disappeared, and people came together to support their fellow Americans in need.

We as human beings must be able to see ourselves as

others see us. Once we have managed to see ourselves in this way, then we must turn inward, to look at ourselves from the inside. If we can see what the stranger can see, and we can look inside of ourselves to see what we do not want to see, then we have positioned ourselves to become better people, as a result of this exercise.

I firmly believe that it is crucial for us as human beings to look at ourselves in terms of humanity and not just in terms of what might be in something for us as individuals.

All great things in life are a blending of the process and the journey. Success in life is not a destination; it is a journey.

The process should never stop; and for those of us who have children, it is our responsibility to help them understand these concepts. We as human beings can make a difference; we just have to keep trying.

"Those who cannot remember the past are condemned to repeat it." —

George Santayana (1863–1952), U.S. philosopher, poet.

History is a word that means different things to different people depending on how events had affected them.

For example, white America has one view of the slaughter of the Native American Indians. And, the Indians whose ancestors were slaughtered in the millions have a different view of our history. How can a white person truly come to understand that difference? It is a wholly different perspective of the same historical events.

It is important to understand how different people might have a different perspective concerning a matter. It is important for us to be able to see how others might view White Male Privilege, based on how White Male Privilege may or may not affect them.

Here are some examples of differing viewpoints: a rich white male versus a poor white male; a young white male verses an old white male. How do females look at this privilege? How do older females look at it? How about a black female? How about a black man who is a professional? How about a young black man in prison? Is he guilty or not? I could go on and on regarding different scenarios. My point is that there are endless possibilities. It's important to understand the other person's perspective as best as you can.

How does the point of view change between the oppressed and the oppressor? I am not trying to make it sound like I have a degree in psychology, because I don't, but oppressors generally are individuals who live in fear and are insecure with themselves. The only way that they can feel that they have power over their own lives, is to feel that they have power over others. Many oppressors do not even realize their own manipulative behaviors.

Every person I interviewed had quite different perspectives on this subject, based on how White Male Privilege did or did not affect them. From the standpoint of each individual, they saw White Male Privilege exercised in either a political, social or economic realm.

Denial has always played an important role in the perpetuation of White Male Privilege. During the interviews I heard a few times that "it *was* that way, however, now it isn't," or "it's not as bad as it used to be."

My contention is that the new, subtler display of racism is just as bad. Racism in most cases might not be as blatant, however, the backstabbing is still there. The hurt is still inflicted, even if not in their faces. Which is worse, blatant racism or subtle discrimination? It kind of makes you think.

So many people cannot even recognize White Male Privilege, even when it is practiced right under their nose. If people cannot see White Male Privilege in action, how can they point it out or stand against it? They can't, can they?

The Bible says, "If the blind shall lead the blind, both shall fall into the ditch." Matthew 15:14.

Whether done in blindness or denial, allowing racism and discrimination to continue unfettered will allow these damaging practices to retain their power into another generation.

We must open our eyes to the ugliness of racism, discrimination and White Male Privilege. And then, we must educate our young. Privilege or lack of privilege of any kind needs to be addressed in our school systems. It needs to be addressed in our churches. It must be addressed in our homes. If we don't teach our children right from wrong, who will?

It is important to share with our children the understanding that people will see White Male Privilege through the lens of their own personal point of view. Our children must understand that individuals will be directed in their lives according to many factors such as family upbringing, education, economic and political status, race, color, religion and many other factors.

Our children must understand that their friends may not understand racism, discrimination and White Male Privilege in the same way that they do. They must know that these differences do not make them any better than their friends, who do not share the same point of view. Our children must understand that part of their role in the human experience is to teach others right from wrong. They must understand that they have the power to influence other people through their own individual actions.

Our children need to understand that being black does not make one a criminal. They must understand that being black does not make people stupid. They must understand that being white does not give them the right to have privilege over another. Our children must understand that when they see wrong in their schools or in their workplace, they must have the courage to stand up for those who are being oppressed.

It is our responsibility to teach our children to be a shining beacon, pointing the way to right behavior and right actions.

It is our responsibility to take actions in our own lives, and to help our children take actions in their lives, to end the cycle of destruction fueled by racism, discrimination and White Male Privilege.

The words of Francine Armstrong are as pertinent here, as when I used them in a previous chapter: "All men are created equal in the sight of God. Freedom is never free. Social justice must be fought for."

Bibliography

Andersen, Margaret and Collins Patricia (1998). *Race, Class, and Gender: An Anthology* Wadsworth Publishing Company (pp.11 - 19)

Davis-Adeshote, Jeanette (1995) *Black Survival in White America: From Past History to the Next Century.* Bryant and Dillon Publishers. Inc.

Elder, Larry (2000) *The Ten Things You Can't Say In America.* St. Martins Press First Edition

Jacobson, Matthew, (1998) *Whiteness of a Different Color: European Immigrants and the Alchemy of Race.* First Harvard Press. (pp13 - 90)

Katz, Judy (1987) *White Awareness Handbook For Anti-Racism Training.* University of Oklahoma Press.

93

Kivel, Paul (1996) *Uprooting Racism.* New Society Publishers. (pp 8 - 16; 50 - 58 & 120 - 130)

Lipset, Seymour (1997) *American Exceptional.* (pp 31 - 150)

Mc Intosh, Peggy (1988) *White Privilege and Male Privilege.* (pp 94 - 105)

Sennett, Richard and Cobb, Jonathan (1993) *The Hidden Injuries of Class.* Norton Paperback

Thoreau, David (1967) *The Variorum Civil Disobedience.* Twayne Publishers. Inc.

Websters New World Dictionary (1988) Third Edition